Chocolate on a Tree

I0159313

Robert Peprah-Gyamfi

Kiddy Kiddy Books

Illustrated by: Jessica Otabil

Published by Kiddy Kiddy Books
www.kiddykiddybooks.com
email: info@kiddykiddybooks.com

ISBN: 978-1-913285-09-8

KIDDY KIDDY BOOKS SERIES No.12

Chocolate on a Tree

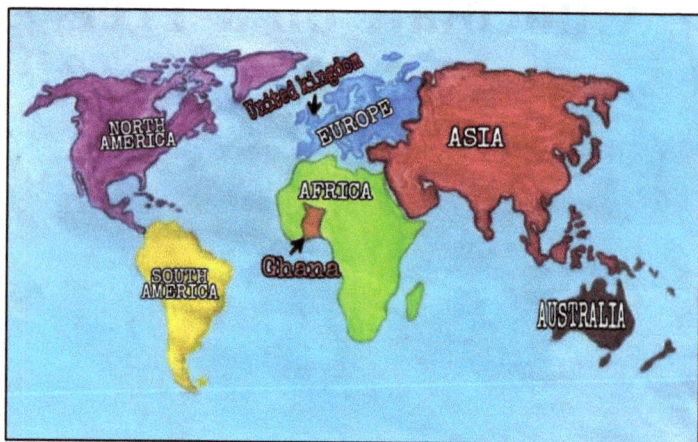

Chocolate on a Tree is part of the KIDDY KIDDY Books Series. The series follows the life of Kofi Mensah, a little boy growing up in Kookookrom, a tiny village in Ghana, West Africa.

Let me tell you about Kofi Mensah. He is seven years old.

He lives in a little village in Ghana, in West Africa. The village is called Kookookrom which means Cocoa Settlement.

He is in Year 2 in the primary school. He has two older brothers.

His parents are farmers but only have two small pieces of land. They have no machines to help them in their hard work on the land.

They grow two types of crops. The first type of crops provides food for the family. There are no grocery shops in the village. Every family has to live on the food they grow on small pieces of land. Examples of the plants they grow for food are plantains, yams, onions and tomatoes.

The second type of crops grown by Kofi's parents are cash crops. They grow them not to eat but to sell. The money from the sale helps support the family.

The main cash crop grown by Kofi's parents is cocoa.

Kofi learnt in school that cocoa is also known as cacao in different parts of the world.

So this story is about cocoa. Kofi wants to tell you what it is like helping his parents on their cocoa farm.

The cocoa seed requires a period of about three to five years to grow into a plant able to bear fruit. The plant needs a fertile soil and plenty of rain and sunshine. At the time they start bearing fruit, the trees are about three to five metres (ten to fifteen feet) tall.

The fruit of the cocoa plant is also called a pod. The cocoa fruit is shaped like an egg.

When the pods first appear on the trees, they are small and green in colour.

As they grow they increase in size. Later the colour of the cocoa pods changes from green to yellow. The yellow pods are ripe and ready to be harvested.

Kofi's father harvests the cocoa pods with the help of a machete. With the help of the machete, he cuts down the cocoa pods growing on the cocoa tree as well as on its branches.

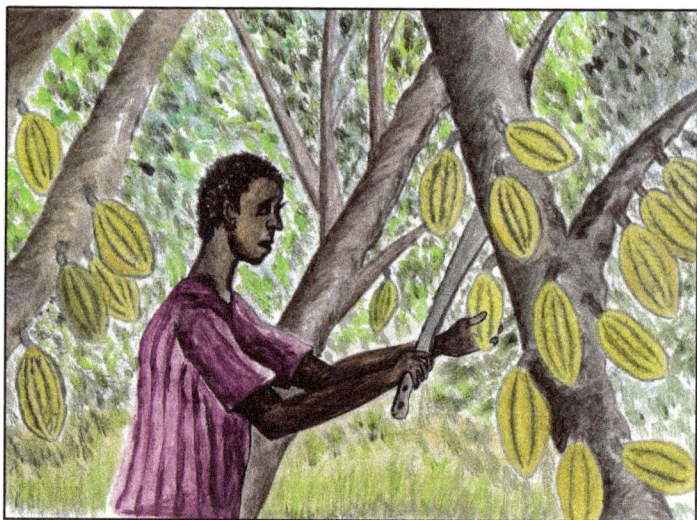

Kofi and the rest of the family collect the cocoa pods that are cut down from the trees. The harvested pods are collected into small groups. Each group contains about six to ten cocoa pods and are about three metres (ten feet apart from each other. Usually, the helpers gather the pods into about a hundred small groups spread all over the farm.

Next, Kofi and the helpers carry the small groups of pods to one single assembly point located on the same farm.

Gathering the pods at a single location on the farm involves much hard work. It would be helpful for Kofi and his family if a vehicle such as a tractor could be used to transport the cocoa beans to this central location. But Kofi's parents are poor. They are unable to purchase or even hire a tractor to help them. So, Kofi and his family have to do the job themselves.

Kofi and the other helpers place six to twelve pods in a basket and carry the baskets on their heads to the collecting point on the farm. Kofi does not have to carry as many pods as the adults. The adults have big baskets. while Kofi only has a small basket.

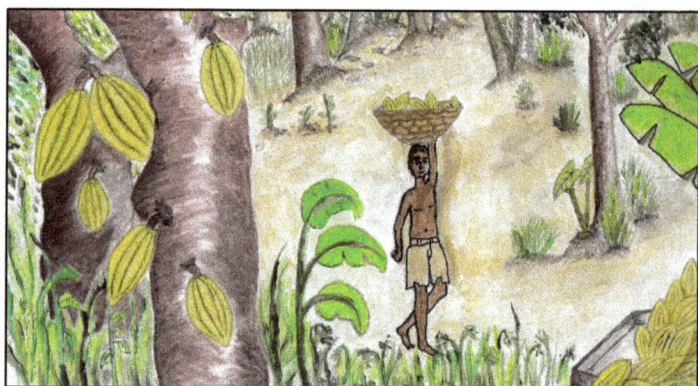

The adults are able to carry up to twelve pods in a basket; Kofi is given a basket with only six pods.

Do you want to know how Kofi is able to balance the load on his head? Kofi's reply is that one day, when he was about five years old, he and his family were getting ready to return home after a long day of work on the farm. He saw that his parents and his older brothers were carrying baskets on their heads. Kofi then turned to his mother and began:

"Mama, please give me something to carry!"

"No, you are too young for the job!" his mother replied.

"No, I will give it a try," he insisted.

"Are you sure?"

"Yes."

His mother then placed a finger of banana on his head.

"Okay boy, try this one."

"Great news!" he shouted with joy.

Kofi walked home without any problems. Since that day, Kofi has been balancing items on his head.

So, Kofi and his family have to carry the cocoa pods to one central location on the farm.

The pods are cut open with the help of a small machete. In order to prevent injury, children like Kofi are not allowed to open the pods themselves.

Each pod contains around twenty seeds. The seeds are covered by a white fruity pulp. The fruity pulp has a sweet taste.

The seeds or beans are separated from the surrounding pulp and gathered together into a heap.

The heap is tightly covered with the broad leaves of banana plants growing on the farm and left on the farm for seven days.

During the seven days, the seeds undergo fermentation. Fermentation? What is that, someone may ask. To put it simply, it is the process whereby molecules or particles are broken down in the absence of oxygen. The fermentation or chemical changes are important because they make the chocolate made from the cocoa beans taste good.

After the beans have been left for seven days to ferment, they are collected and sent home for drying.

Kofi helps carry the beans home for drying. The beans are dried on mats spread on wooden structures built by Kofi's father to help dry the cocoa.

Kofi lives in a hot climate. There is abundant sunshine for most of the year. Kofi learnt at school that there is a special machine for drying cocoa beans. Kofi's father does not have enough money to purchase such a machine, so he depends on sunshine to dry his beans.

The cocoa beans take between seven and fourteen days to dry. Kofi's father sells his dried cocoa beans to a company that specialises in the purchase of dried cocoa beans from farmers around the country. The company has a branch in the village. For ease of transporting the dried beans for sale, they are filled into sacks made of strong material such as the fibre of the jute plant.

Kofi's father supports his family with the money he obtains from the sale of his cocoa beans

The company that purchases the dried cocoa beans from the farmers in the village then stores the sacks filled with the dried cocoa in a large warehouse. Kofi can still remember the time when the building was put up. He was four years old at the time. He was excited to see the huge bulldozers and the other earth-moving machines at work. It took about twelve months to complete the building.

From time to time, big lorries arrive in the village to carry away the sacks filled with the dried cocoa beans.

Kofi wanted to know what happened to the cocoa beans taken out of the village so he asked his parents.

"No idea!" they told him.

One day as he walked along the street in the small village, Kofi met Mr Asante. He is the clerk employed to purchase cocoa beans in the village.

"Good day, Mr Asante," he greeted him politely.

"Good day, Kofi," Mr Asante replied. "How can I help you?"

"Tell me, Sir, where do the huge lorries that come to collect the sacks filled with cocoa beans take them to?"

"To the port at Tema."

"Tema? I have never heard the name!"

"Well, it is a large town located about twenty miles (thirty kilometres) to the east of Accra, our capital city."

"What happens when the cocoa beans get to the port?"

"They are exported."

"So nothing remains in our country?"

"Only a small portion, less than five percent, my dear."

"And what are cocoa beans good for?"

"They are used to produce several items, including chocolate."

"Chocolate? What is chocolate?"

"You have no idea what chocolate is?

"No. Never heard the name!"

"So, you have been helping your Papa grow cocoa beans all these years and you have no idea of chocolate?"

"No, Sir."
"Ach, how do I explain it to your understanding?'

Mr Asante paused for a while.

"Okay, I will try," he began. "Chocolate is a paste. It is obtained after the cocoa beans have been roasted and ground."

"The cocoa beans are roasted? How does that happen?"

"You are asking me tough questions, Kofi! I have been told there are big machines that help to roast the cocoa beans and also grind them. I have never seen them myself. To give you an idea what chocolate looks like, I will bring you a chocolate bar next time I travel to Makokrom, the nearest big town. They are on sale in some of the grocery shops there."

"What is a chocolate bar?"

"It is a delicious sweet made from chocolate paste."

"That is really nice of you! I cannot wait to try it!"

"I will surely keep my promise."

"Thank you very much."

"You are welcome. Goodbye, Kofi."

"Goodbye, Mr Asante."

As Kofi lay in bed that night, he kept thinking about his conversation with Mr Asante. He looked forward to the day when he would have his first taste of chocolate.

Soon he was lost in sleep!

Look out for more exciting stories about the life experiences of Kofi Mensah, the little boy from Kookookrom, in Ghana, West Africa.

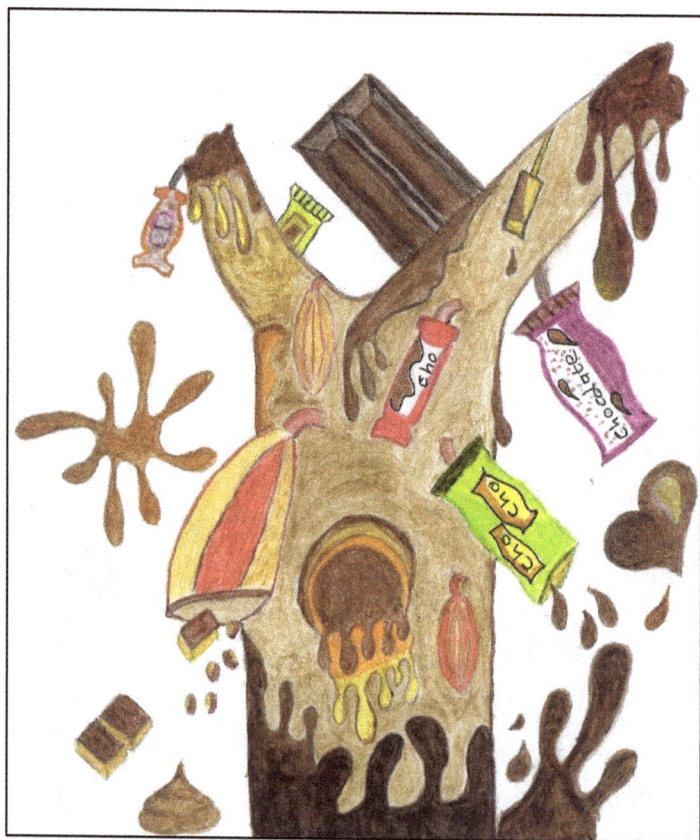

GLOSSARY

Accra   Capital city of Ghana.

Cash crops   Crops grown by a family not to eat, but to sell.

Cocoa   Also known as cacao. Used to make chocolate.

Fermentation   Chemical process when the molecules are broken down without using oxygen. Makes the chocolate taste good.

Ghana   A country in West Africa.

Jute   Fibrous plant used to make hessian sacks.

Kofi   Boy's name, meaning born on a Friday.

Kookookrom   Name of Kofi's village, meaning Cocoa Settlement.

Machete   Broad-bladed tool like an axe used in farming.

Makokrom   Nearest big town to Kookookrom. Means Pepper Settlement.

Mensah	If parents give birth to a boy, to be followed directly by a boy and yet another boy, the third boy is called Mensah.
Plantain	Looks like a green banana, but is treated as a vegetable and cooked.
Plantation	Estate on which crops such as cocoa are grown.
Pod	Fruit of the cocoa plant, shaped like an egg.
Pulp	The soft, moist inner part of a fruit.
Cocoa seed	After 3-5 years, grows into a plant able to bear fruit.
Tema	A large town and port 30km (20miles) to the east of Accra.
Warehouse	A large building for storing goods.
Yam	A vegetable like a potato, which can be boiled, roasted or fried.

ABOUT THE AUTHOR

Dr. Robert Peprah-Gyamfi grew up in Mpintimpi, a little village in Ghana, West Africa.

He faced many challenges growing up in that impoverished village. Despite the challenging living conditions he faced growing up in that impoverished village, he later made it to the Hannover Medical School in Germany, where he qualified as a doctor in 1992.

Robert now works part -time as a doctor and spends the rest of his time writing. Indeed, he has been a passionate storyteller from a young age. He started his first novel as a teenager, but could not however finish his work due to lack of resources.

Robert, who regards himself as citizen of the Global Village, is currently resident in the UK.

To connect with him please visit: www.kiddykiddybooks.com